Is
TIME
TRAVEL
Possible?

Nick Hunter

raintree

Raintree is an imprint of Capstone Global Library
Limited, a company incorporated in England and Wales
having its registered office at 264 Banbury Road, Oxford,
OX2 7DY– Registered company number: 6695582

www.raintree.co.uk
myorders@raintree.co.uk

Edited by Helen Cox Cannons
Designed by Steve Mead
Original illustrations © Capstone Global Library Ltd 2016
Picture research by Kelly Garvin
Production by Victoria Fitzgerald
Originated by Capstone Global Library Ltd
Printed and bound in China

ISBN 978 1 4747 1476 1 (hardback)
19 18 17 16 15
10 9 8 7 6 5 4 3 2 1

ISBN 978 1 4747 1494 5 (paperback)
20 19 18 17 16
10 9 8 7 6 5 4 3 2 1

British Library Cataloguing in Publication Data
A full catalogue record for this book is available from the
British Library.

Acknowledgements
Alamy: A.F. Archive, 5 (bottom), 11 (middle),
GeoPic, 10 (bottom right); Corbis: Bettmann, 8 (b),
Christophe Vander Eecken, 30 (m); Getty Images:
UniversalImagesGroup, 17 (br), Warner Bros, 38 (b);
NASA/Kim Shiflett, 20 (bottom left); Newscom/SNAP/
REX, 39 (m); Science Source: 9 (m), 15 (b), 16 (b), 41,
Andrew Brookes/National Physical Laboratory, 7 (top
right), Detlev van Ravenswaay, 24 (b), Lynette Cook,
25 (b); Shutterstock: absolutimages, 34 (b), agsandrew,
32-33 (background), andrey_I, 26 (m), Bruce Rolff, 8-9
(background), Colleen E. Scott/Scott Designs, 33 (tr),
David Orcea, 38-39, 40 (background), Deniseus, 28 (top
left), Designua, 14 (b), F. Schmidt, 10-11 (background),
Featureflash, 35 (bottom right), John A. Davis, 6 (b),
jupeart, 20-21 (background), kentoh, 18-19 (background),
Kev Draws, 31 (b), koya979, 18 (b), Kritchanut, 8 (tr),
ledinka, 13 (top), Lev Savitskiy, 36 (b), LiliGraphie, 32
(b), Lukas Rs, 30-31 (background), M. Cornelius, 29 (b),
MarcelClemens, 22 (m), Markus Gann, 19 (b), Martina
Vaculikova, 36-37 (background), Nejron Photo, 34 (tr),
pixelparticle, 16-17 (background), Poprotskiy Alexey,
34-35 (background), Rawpixel, 14-15 (background),
serazetdinov, 12 (tl), Sergey Nivens, 6-7 (background),
VLADGRIN, 26 (background), 36, (t), Vladimir
Zadvinskii, 28-29 (background), wavebreakmedia, 40
(b), xfox01, 21 (mr); Wikimedia: ESO/L.Calcada, 28 (bl),
NASA ESA, H. Teplitz and M. Rafelski (IPAC/Caltech),
A. Koekemoer (STScI), R. Windhorst (Arizona State
University), and Z. Levay (STScI), 12 (b), NASA/Les
Bossinas, 27 (b); www.imaginaryfoundation.com, cover

Artistic elements: Shutterstock: agsandrew, Bruce Rolff,
Eky Studio, Maksim Kabakou, Nik Merkulov

We would like to thank Dr Andrew Hanson, Outreach
Manager at the National Physical Laboratory, for his
invaluable help in the preparation of this book.

CONTENTS

MISSION IMPOSSIBLE

Welcome! I'm glad you could come. I'm the Mystery Master. I'm here to clear up conundrums, probe puzzles and explain the unexplained. I've been looking for someone like you for a while.

Have you ever wondered what it would be like to travel through time? Imagine if you could go back and talk to the people who made history, or take a journey forward in time to find out what the future has in store. Time travel would certainly help in solving mysteries.

Your mission is to use all the available evidence to try to solve this scientific puzzle once and for all:

IS TIME TRAVEL POSSIBLE?

Would you like to time travel?
Films and TV programmes make time travel look easy. Characters jump into a time machine, type in the coordinates for the place and time they want to visit and off they go. The journey home is often just as straightforward.

Real time travel would be a lot more complicated than that. An actual time machine would have to test some of science's most mind-boggling theories. Technology is nowhere near giving us the tools we need to really travel to the future or the past, but that doesn't mean it's impossible.

INVESTIGATION TIPS

WARNING!
Unless you meet someone who claims to have travelled through time, you're not going to be interviewing witnesses to solve this mystery. Instead, scientists and their theories have the answers to this big question, and they don't all agree. Do they make sense and can they be confirmed by experiments? Find out as much as you can about the science of time travel.

Creators of films and TV shows often try to imagine what a time machine would look like.

How to be a Super Scientist

The idea of travelling through time may seem crazy, but investigating this mystery is really about understanding and applying the laws of science. Some of the most brilliant scientists in history have worked on this problem, from Albert Einstein to Stephen Hawking, so you're following in some pretty famous footsteps.

The secret to being a good scientist is to be constantly curious about the world around you. If you don't understand how or why something works, ask questions and find the answers.

Astronomers studying distant stars and galaxies try to solve questions about time itself using telescopes.

Don't ask why, ask why not

For scientists, answers to questions about the world should always be based on evidence. So, if someone asks if time travel is possible, you need to find a reason why it could not happen before you can say it's definitely not possible.

Scientists follow a four-step method:

1 What do we want to learn or find out? In this case, we want to know if time travel is possible.

2 Hypothesis: Based on what you know or can find out from research, come up with an idea or reason why it would or would not be possible.

3 Experiment: Design a test or procedure to see whether your hypothesis is correct.

4 Analyse your results and reach your conclusion.

The point of this scientific method is to make sure that personal ideas and bias do not influence your conclusions, which is good advice for any detective.

Super-accurate atomic clocks work by measuring the movements of atoms of Caesium. Atomic clocks are more accurate than the old method of measuring time, using Earth's journey around the Sun.

INVESTIGATION TIPS

Time-travel tools

If you want to find the answer to this scientific secret, you'll need some complex technology:

- A super-accurate clock to measure time: Atomic clocks are the most accurate timepieces on Earth, expected to lose only 1 second every 14 billion years.

- The world's fastest spacecraft: If you could travel close to the speed of light, you may have a chance of time travel. The bad news is that no existing spacecraft could travel close to that speed.

Whose idea was time travel anyway?

To find out who first came up with the idea of time travel, we'd have to travel back in time ourselves. Many ancient texts and folk tales have examples of time travel, including early Hindu and Christian texts.

Time travel stories were told in many different cultures. They include the North American tale of Rip Van Winkle (published around 1820), who falls asleep and wakes up to find himself 20 years in the future. The ancient Japanese story of Urashima Taro is about a fisherman who visits an undersea palace. When he returns home, 300 years have passed. The folk tales usually dealt with travel to the future.

The story of Rip Van Winkle was based on several European and American folk tales about time travel.

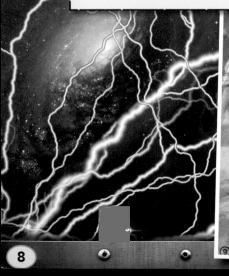
(9)

Science fiction

In the 1800s, interest in time travel continued to grow, as more of the secrets of science were uncovered. Science fiction writers started to use stories to explore scientific ideas, for example, the idea that humans could build a time machine to help them travel through time.

Ancient times

Don't spend too much time worrying about ancient myths of time travel. It was not until the 16th century that humans discovered that Earth orbited around the Sun, although the year that this journey takes was divided into 365 days with an extra day every four years in Roman times.

This astronomical clock tower was built in China around 1,000 years ago. It used water to rotate a globe that mapped the positions of stars and planets.

THE SCIENCE

Who invented time?

From the earliest times, humans were aware of the patterns of day and night and the seasons, even if they did not know that these patterns were set by Earth's journey around the Sun. The ancient Sumerians built the first cities. They were probably the first people to divide the day into the 24 hours containing 60 minutes and 60 seconds that we use today.

THE TIME MACHINE

In 1895, H.G. Wells published *The Time Machine*. His book changed the way people thought about time travel. It tells the story of the Time Traveller, who builds a machine that transports him thousands of years into the future. Other stories from the late 1800s told the story of travellers journeying back in time.

Wells published his amazing tale in an era when technology was changing the world. Motor vehicles had just been invented and the first powered flight by the Wright Brothers was just a few years away. Surely the next step could be time travel?

THE
TIME MACHINE
H. G. WELLS

with an introduction by DONALD WOLLHEIM

COMPLETE AND UNABRIDGED

The illustration on this cover of H.G. Wells's book gives an old-fashioned idea of what people thought a time machine would look like.

Time travel on film

Since the late 1800s, science fiction writers and filmmakers have continued to explore the possibilities of time travel. In the *Back to the Future* films (1985, 1989 and 1990), Marty McFly travels through time in a time machine made from a car. The TV series *Doctor Who*, which began in 1963, shows the adventures of the Doctor as he travels through time in his TARDIS. TARDIS stands for Time and Relative Dimension in Space.

The question you need to answer is: do any of these stories about time travel have any basis in reality? Could they ever come true? To answer that question, we need to look at the very nature of time itself.

The *Back to the Future* films were great fun, but also explored puzzles such as what would happen if someone travelled back in time and changed the past.

TOP SECRET

Carl Sagan was a celebrated physicist who explored his ideas about time travel using science fiction. In his book *Contact*, humans contact an alien civilization by travelling through a tunnel in space, called a wormhole. Find out more about wormholes on page 24.

THE EVIDENCE:
We are all time travellers

It is very difficult to say for certain what time actually is. We could say it is the thing that stops everything happening together. We can measure it but, once a moment is in the past, we cannot recapture it and the future does not yet exist. The only piece of time we can really "touch" is the present moment, which instantly becomes the past. Are you confused yet? These are the kind of ideas we'll have to grapple with if we're going to solve this mystery.

If you think about it, we're all travelling through time. We don't call it time travel because we're all travelling in the same direction at the same speed, at one hour every hour. If we could alter the speed of our journey, that would be what we think of as time travel.

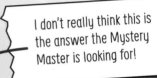

I don't really think this is the answer the Mystery Master is looking for!

The Hubble Space Telescope has enabled humans to see distant galaxies. Light from this area, called the Hubble Ultra Deep Field, takes 13 billion years to reach us. The light started its journey soon after the Universe began.

Nothing we know about can travel faster than light, but light still takes billions of years to reach us from the furthest stars and galaxies.

However, when we look at the stars in the sky, we are looking directly into the past. The light from distant stars can take thousands or millions of years to reach us because of the vast distances in space. The mind-boggling vastness of space could hold the key to this mystery.

TOP SECRET

Years, days, hours, minutes and seconds were invented by humans, based on the rotation of Earth and its journey around the Sun. If there were a civilization somewhere else in the Universe, they would certainly measure time in a very different way.

INVESTIGATION TIPS

Changing our journey

We're actually trying to find out if we can change the way we travel through time, making our journey faster or slower. If we want to go back in time, we would have to reverse the journey completely.

TIME ZONE TRICKERY

If you've ever travelled in a plane across an ocean or continent, you've probably experienced something like time travel. If you fly from Europe to North America, your flight may last for seven hours but, when you land, the clocks show a time only a couple of hours later than when you took off. Have you travelled through time?

TOP SECRET

The International Date Line is an imaginary line in the middle of the Pacific Ocean. If you cross this line from east to west, you are moving on by a whole day, so you'd move from midday on Tuesday to midday on Wednesday.

Standard time zones of the world

This map shows how the world is divided into time zones. Zero is known as Greenwich Mean Time.

Your body may feel like you've travelled through time, but this doesn't really count. Earth's surface is divided into different time zones so when, for example, it is 12 o'clock midday in London, it is 7 o'clock in the morning in New York City, USA. This is because Earth is spinning on its axis and the Sun seems to rise in the sky earlier in London than it does in New York. The time zones are just a human invention to ensure that noon is approximately the time when the sun is highest in the sky wherever you are in the world.

However, the reason you can cross several time zones in a day is down to your speed of travel at just under 1,000 kilometres (621 miles) per hour in a passenger jet aircraft. Speed, or velocity to give it its scientific name, does have a lot to do with the possibilities of time travel.

THE SCIENCE

Clocks in space

While crossing time zones is not really time travel, clocks on fast-moving aircraft or spacecraft do run very slightly slower than a clock on Earth's surface. A clock on the International Space Station (below), orbiting Earth at a height of 353 kilometres (220 miles) ticks about 0.0000000014 per cent slower than the clocks on Earth. After six months in space, an astronaut on the International Space Station will have aged about 0.007 seconds less than people on Earth.

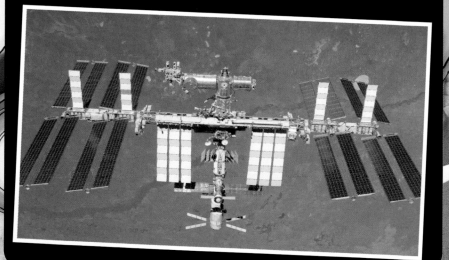

INTO THE
FOURTH DIMENSION

H.G. Wells was one of the first people to describe time as the fourth dimension, alongside the three physical dimensions length, breadth and thickness. When Wells wrote *The Time Machine*, the idea that anyone could travel through time was impossible, but one remarkable scientist was about to start work on solving the problem.

Key witness?
Einstein's the person we should be talking to. His ideas changed science forever, and he came up with many of his most important theories while working in an office, not a laboratory.

This guy Einstein is a big part of this investigation. Here are some things you need to know about him.

NAME: ALBERT EINSTEIN

BORN: 14 March 1879, Ulm, Germany

EDUCATION: Luitpold Gymnasium, Munich, Germany; Swiss Federal Polytechnic School, Zurich, Switzerland

CAREER:

- 1905: While working as technical assistant at the Swiss Patent Office, Einstein publishes four scientific papers that change the course of science, including one on the Special Theory of Relativity

Turn the page to find out more about Einstein's incredible ideas!

- 1914: Appointed Director of Kaiser Wilhelm Institute for Physics in Berlin, Germany

- 1915: Publishes several papers on the General Theory of Relativity (see pages 18 and 19), explaining how gravity holds the Universe together and shapes space–time

- 1933: Leaves Germany to settle in the United States. Einstein was Jewish, and was threatened by the anti-Jewish policies of German leader Adolf Hitler.

- Becomes very active as a campaigner for peace and the Jewish state of Israel

AWARDS: Nobel Prize for Physics 1921, *Time* Magazine Person of the Century

DIED: 18 April 1955, Princeton, New Jersey, USA

TOP SECRET

At school, it was clear that Einstein was brilliant at maths but he was less interested in other subjects and found the discipline of school life difficult. One teacher said that the young genius would never amount to anything!

Relatively speaking

Albert Einstein was not even 30 years old when he came up with a theory which many scientists think shows that time travel is possible. It's called the Special Theory of Relativity, and it changed our understanding of how the Universe fits together.

In his research papers *Special Relativity* and his later *General Theory of Relativity*, Einstein concluded that nothing in the Universe could travel faster than light. Einstein's theory states that space and time are really two aspects of the same thing and that an object travelling close to the speed of light can *warp*, or bend, space and time.

Einstein concluded that massive objects such as stars and planets could bend space because of their gravitational fields. This warping of space could also affect time.

Special Relativity is based on the idea that light always appears to travel at the same speed, no matter how fast the observer is moving. This idea had already been proved by measuring the time it took the Sun's light to reach the moving Earth.

If you were in a spacecraft travelling close to the speed of light, time would pass more slowly for you than it would outside the spacecraft. In theory, this means you could travel forward in time. But it would require an almost endless amount of energy to make an object travel that fast.

Einstein's theory also gave rise to the famous equation:

E=mc²

This states that the energy of an object (E) is equal to its mass (m) multiplied by the speed of light squared (c²).

INVESTIGATION TIPS

Prove it!
Einstein's ideas seemed incredible when he first revealed them. But scientists have carried out many experiments since then that prove he was right. We can't see or measure space–time, but we can see the effects it has on objects in space and how we view them from Earth.

During a solar eclipse in 1919, astronomers proved that light could be bent by massive objects such as the Sun. This was claimed by Einstein in his General Theory of Relativity.

TRAVELLING CLOSE TO LIGHT SPEED

Einstein's *Special Relativity* and *General Theory of Relativity* tell us that time travel may be possible within the laws of physics. If an astronaut could travel close to the speed of light, then time would run much more slowly from their point of view thanks to Special Relativity. Also, being in places of different gravitational forces changes the speed of the passage of time through General Relativity. Both these approaches would make travel into the future possible.

Warp speed

Most scientists think it's impossible to travel faster than light because it takes so much energy to get even close to it, and an infinite amount to get anything with mass to travel at light speed. In 2018, the National Aeronautics and Space Administration (NASA) will launch the Solar Probe Plus to orbit the Sun. This will be the fastest human-made object in history, travelling at speeds of 200 kilometres per second (125 miles per second). That's impressive, but it's less than 1 per cent of the speed of light.

Spacecraft such as this require huge quantities of energy to reach the speed needed to escape the pull of Earth's gravity.

THE SCIENCE

Speed of light

The speed of light is 299,792 kilometres per second (186,282 miles per second). This means that light can travel 7.5 times around the Equator in one second.

Nothing can travel faster than light in a vacuum, but would it be possible to design a spacecraft that could travel anywhere close to the speed of light? Even if we could build a spacecraft that would be able to travel at close to light speed without being destroyed, Einstein's work makes clear that accelerating an object close to light speed would require an incredibly large amount of energy. If such a thing is possible, it is beyond our current technology to achieve it.

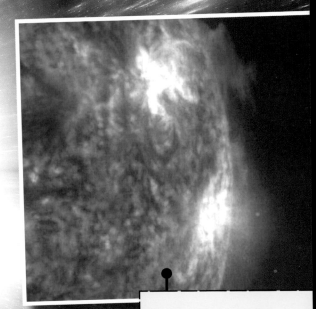

The most powerful source of energy we know is the nuclear fusion that happens inside the Sun and other stars. One day, it may be possible to harness this source to power spacecraft through space and time.

INVESTIGATION TIPS

Logical thinking

Always ask the tough questions. It may be true that time travel is possible within the laws of physics, as shown by Einstein, but always think about what technology would be needed to achieve it. Travelling to the future seems challenging enough, but going into the past could be impossible.

BLACK HOLES

Black holes are not really holes – they were once called invisible stars. When a star runs out of fuel to keep it burning, the force of gravity takes over. The star becomes a densely packed core of matter. The more mass there is in an object, the greater the gravitational force it exerts on the space around it. The collapsed star has such a strong gravitational field that even light cannot escape from it, so it becomes a black hole.

Gas and other matter swirls around the black hole at the centre of this picture. It reaches speeds close to the speed of light as it is pulled towards the black hole.

THE SCIENCE

Finding black holes

Black holes appear completely dark, but astronomers can detect them by examining how they affect stars and other bodies.

Twisting time

Close to a black hole, strange things happen to space and time, as explained by Einstein's General Theory of Relativity. If you were in a spaceship heading towards a black hole, the force of gravity would cause the ship to accelerate dramatically until it reached almost the speed of light.

At that point, you would have reached the event horizon. This is the point at which the black hole's gravity is so strong that nothing could escape. The good news is that, as you reach these incredible speeds, the black hole warps space and time, so time would seem to stretch out in comparison to normal time. Although you'd be increasingly hurtling towards your death, were anyone able to see you from outside (which they can't because no light is coming from you) you would appear to them to be slowing down the closer you got to the centre. The bad news is that, before reaching the event horizon, time wouldn't slow down as far as you were concerned, and you and your spacecraft would be ripped apart by the gigantic forces.

INVESTIGATION TIPS

Keep a safe distance

Don't try investigating a black hole up close – it could get very messy! It's not a problem you're likely to have, as the nearest black hole to Earth is about 1,600 light years away. A light year is the distance that light travels in a year.

The event horizon is the point where the gravitational pull of the black hole is so strong that not even light can escape.

EVENT HORIZON

The centre of a black hole contains all the mass from the star that was created, compressed in an infinitely small space.

Scientists believe that a black hole is structured in this way.

Light rays are bent as they get close to the event horizon of the black hole.

No object would be able to withstand the extreme stretching once it crossed the event horizon.

Wormholes and cosmic string

Black holes seem unbelievable but scientists are sure they exist. Some of the other secrets of the Universe are still just theories, but they could hold the key to time travel.

Wormholes

One of Einstein's wildest ideas was the existence of wormholes. Scientists were divided on what the centre of a black hole looked like. In 1935, Einstein suggested that the extreme bending of space and time that takes place at the centre of a black hole could be explained by a bridge or hole. These bridges could be shortcuts to other parts of space and time, or to a parallel Universe almost identical to our own.

More recently, scientists have explored whether we could produce our own wormhole, creating short cuts to other places in space and time. This is not practical now but may be possible one day.

Wormholes could be portals to distant parts of space and different points in time. A wormhole is much like a tunnel with two ends, as shown here. Each end is a separate point in space-time.

THE SCIENCE

Wormhole reality

Wormholes sound like a good solution, but no one has found one yet. If they do exist, natural wormholes are almost certainly incredibly tiny. Making them big enough to travel through would be almost impossible, and would release huge amounts of deadly radiation.

Cosmic string

Cosmic string is matter that was left over from the birth of the Universe. Scientists do not all agree on what it's like, or even whether it exists at all. Cosmic string could enable us to bend space and time to make time travel possible. Cosmic string's huge mass means it has a powerful gravitational field. If astronomers can find identical galaxies they may be able to prove that cosmic string exists.

TOP SECRET

Cosmic string is believed to contain so much mass packed together that one cubic millimetre would weigh a million billion tonnes.

This is an artist's impression of cosmic string. Scientists believe it has such powerful gravity that it could bend light to create a mirror image of a galaxy.

Building a time machine

There may be ways of travelling through time, but you'll need to build a spacecraft or some kind of machine to help you achieve it. A modified car or an old police box won't really deal with the extreme velocity and forces you'll have to overcome.

To make a time machine, scientists would have to generate enough force to warp space itself.

Some scientists have suggested ways of building a time machine by creating an enormous cylinder in space rotating at incredibly high speeds. This could warp space and time to create a time loop that would make it possible to travel through time. American physicist Frank Tipler developed a plan for a time machine like this in 1974.

He said that the cylinder would need to be 100 kilometres (62 miles) long and 10 kilometres (6 miles) wide. Tipler wasn't sure it would work, even if science could overcome the practical issue of making it and sending it into space.

First, make a wormhole ...

A human-made wormhole may be another way of creating a time machine. The steps to achieve this would be challenging, to say the least:

1. Create a working wormhole, big enough for a human to pass through.
2. Find a way of transporting one mouth of the wormhole on a spacecraft. The other mouth would stay on Earth.
3. Launch the spacecraft and travel close to the speed of light so there is a time difference between the two mouths of the wormhole.
4. Use the wormhole to travel between two points in time.

A working time machine?

Do you think any of these ideas would be possible?

- Tipler's giant cylinder would have to be incredibly strong and able to spin round thousands of times every second ... in space!
- The idea of creating and transporting a large wormhole at very high speed relies on major changes in technology. Scientists are not even sure if wormholes exist!

An artist's impression of a spacecraft travelling through a wormhole. Making this a reality might, at best, occur in the distant future.

Alien visitors

Our search for the secrets of time travel has taken us into deep space. Maybe we're not the only ones looking for answers to this mystery. Is it possible that somewhere in the Universe, an advanced civilization has already found the answer?

UFO time machines

Have you ever seen a UFO, which is short for Unidentified Flying Object? This means any object flying through the sky that cannot be identified. Many UFOs have later turned out to be experimental aircraft or unusually shaped clouds, but many people believe they have seen alien spacecraft. They describe spacecraft travelling at very high speeds, suddenly appearing and disappearing.

If distant planets were home to advanced civilizations, they would need to have unlocked the secrets of wormholes or travel at light speed to visit Earth.

Astronomers are constantly scanning the skies to find Earth-like planets orbiting distant stars that could support life. As there are billions of stars and planets in the Universe, it is quite possible that intelligent life is out there somewhere. If time travel is possible, maybe alien beings have already discovered how to cross space and time.

Where's the evidence?

Some people claim that debris from crashed spacecraft has been found. Other people even believe aliens have abducted them. However, scientists have not yet discovered proof that intelligent alien life exists or has existed in the past, let alone whether aliens can travel through time.

If we believe UFOs do carry travellers across time and space, and they're not visitors from another planet, who could they be? They could be visitors from our future.

This picture is not real, but some people believe that the secrets of time travel may have already been revealed in some top secret desert location.

Time travel at CERN

If you know where to look, you'll find many scientists investigating the outer limits of scientific knowledge. The CERN laboratory near Geneva in Switzerland is the place to start looking. This is where scientists from across the world explore the origins of the Universe and the tiny particles that make up all matter.

CERN is home to the Large Hadron Collider. This is a 27-kilometre (17-mile) long tunnel buried underground. In this tunnel, beams made up of incredibly tiny particles are accelerated so the particles are travelling around the tunnel 11,000 times every second, close to the speed of light.

The Large Hadron Collider recreates the conditions just after the Big Bang, but on a tiny scale.

TOP SECRET

Powerful magnets are used to direct the particles around the Large Hadron Collider. Could magnetism help to accelerate larger objects close to the speed of light?

We know that anything reaching these speeds can behave very strangely. Some scientists think that the Large Hadron Collider could be the first working time machine. Particles moving close to light speed may move back and forward in time, although no positive results have so far been found.

If we can get tiny particles to move at this speed, could it work with larger objects?

THE SCIENCE

What is the Large Hadron Collider for?

The Large Hadron Collider is designed to try to recreate the conditions when the Universe formed more than 13 billion years ago, in a gigantic explosion called the Big Bang. Beams of particles collide at ultra high speeds so that scientists can explore the results.

This is a simple model of an atom. Physicists at CERN are working with the tiny particles that make up atoms. Around 100,000 atoms would fit across the width of a human hair.

PUZZLES AND PARADOXES

Just as scientists try to prove that time travel could be possible, they also look for reasons why it won't work. If it really were possible to build a time machine, we would still need to solve some of the other problems, or paradoxes, that any time traveller would face. Try to get your head round these tricky situations.

The Grandfather Paradox

Imagine you could travel into the past. You meet your grandfather but somehow prevent him from meeting your grandmother. As a result, your mother is never born, and neither are you. If you weren't born, you couldn't have travelled to the past in the first place.

If you went back to the past and changed one thing in your ancestors' lives, it could result in you never being born!

Possible solutions:
- Since you were born and able to travel back, it is not possible for you to alter history.
- Some scientists believe there might be several parallel Universes. If you travel back in time and alter history, an alternative future would happen in another Universe.

This is impossible to prove without a working time machine.

Copying yourself

What if you had a time machine and travelled 10 minutes into the past to meet a slightly younger version of yourself? Together, the two versions of you travel into the past to meet a third version of yourself. For one person to become three instantly would involve creating mass and energy from nothing, which is against the laws of science.

Do these puzzles convince you that time travel to the past could never work, or are they just questions to be solved once we have developed a time machine?

Travelling back in time creates many more problems than a journey into the future.

THE SCIENCE

Time limits

Even time travel's biggest supporters accept that we could not travel back in time before the invention of the time machine. A time machine would have to link different points in space–time and it would be impossible to link to a time when the machine did not exist.

WHERE ARE ALL THE TIME TOURISTS?

wish you were here!

Have you ever met someone from the future? If someone could prove they came from the future, it would be the ultimate evidence that time travel is possible. However, if time tourists are walking among us, they've managed to keep it secret.

If you could travel back in time, would you tell anyone? Would you use your secret knowledge of the future to get rich or alter history?

There are, of course, advantages for time travellers in keeping their journey secret. They'd already know the winning lottery numbers. Someone who knew exactly what was going to happen in the future would have enormous power over businesses, governments and others. However, if they used this knowledge, the future could be altered.

Limits of time travel

Of course, the other explanation is that time travel to the past is just not possible, or that no one can travel back before the invention of the time machine. If you could design a working time machine, you might be visited by lots of time tourists who come to visit the inventor who solved this great mystery.

THE SCIENCE

The party's over

On 28 June 2009, Professor Stephen Hawking (below) held a party at Cambridge University. Guests at the party were greeted with a banner that read "Welcome time travellers!" The twist was that Hawking did not tell anyone about his party until after it had happened. Only a true time traveller could have known about it and travelled from the future to be there. Nobody came.

Making sense of it all

Now you've seen what the scientists say about the possibilities of time travel, it's time to make up your own mind. The Mystery Master is looking for answers. Will we be able to jet off to the future or zoom back to the past?

Scientists are still unravelling the mysteries of distant galaxies and incredible areas of the Universe, such as black holes.

The evidence in favour of time travel all goes back to Albert Einstein and his theories about space and time. At first, his ideas contradicted the views of most scientists and everyday observations, but scientific experiments and observations have proved that Einstein's theories about the Universe were correct.

Past and future

There is much more scientific evidence about the possibilities of travel to the future, as we know that time passes more slowly if you travel at very high speeds or get close to heavy objects whose gravity makes you weigh more than you are now. Travel to the past seems to be much more difficult and raises many more questions.

Time and technology

If you think that time travel is possible according to the laws of science, we then have to solve the technology issues. Could we ever develop a spacecraft that could travel close to light speed or tame wormholes? Einstein published his theories just two years after the Wright Brothers made the first flight in a powered aircraft. Space travel was just a distant dream, but within a few decades astronauts walked on the Moon. The technology of time travel is a long way away but is it impossible?

I know scientists say there's no reason why time travel should be impossible, but that doesn't mean we can all start voyaging through space and time in a rocket-powered sports car. Let's look at the other side of the argument. There are many theories about wormholes and cosmic string, but we don't know the whole truth about these things, and it's possible they don't even exist.

Will we ever solve this mystery?

Scientists take the view that something is possible, unless they can prove that it is not possible. The mysteries of time travel will be solved if scientists find proof that it is against the laws of physics. In more than 100 years since he first published the *Special Theory of Relativity*, Einstein's ideas about space and time have been backed up.

If humans do ever invent a time machine, it will probably look nothing like the versions imagined by Hollywood filmmakers.

However, that does not mean that the mysteries of time travel will be solved in the near future. The best way to solve this puzzle once and for all would be for someone to build a working time machine. At the moment, time machines are still restricted to science fiction. Ideas such as Tipler's giant spinning cylinder in space are not possible with current technology, but technology changes fast. A new discovery or invention could one day make a time machine a realistic goal.

The TV series *Star Trek* followed the voyages of humans exploring deep space. So far, astronauts have only visited the Moon.

TOP SECRET

The nearest star to Earth after the Sun is 4.2 light years away, so it would take four years to travel there at the speed of light. Incredible things like black holes and possible wormholes are much further away.

Even if you could travel close to the speed of light, the Universe is so huge that it would make it very difficult to use a black hole or wormhole for time travel. It may be possible for humans to create a wormhole, but that technology is a long way away.

Solving the puzzles

You should also think about what would happen if time travel were possible. What if we could travel back in time and change the past? Some scientists believe there are different parallel Universes to allow for this. Why have we not been visited by time tourists from the future, or are they here and we just don't know about it?

How will we know?

We will only know if time travel is successful if someone or something can be transported into the past. If time travel to the future is a reality, we may never know, or at least not until after it's happened.

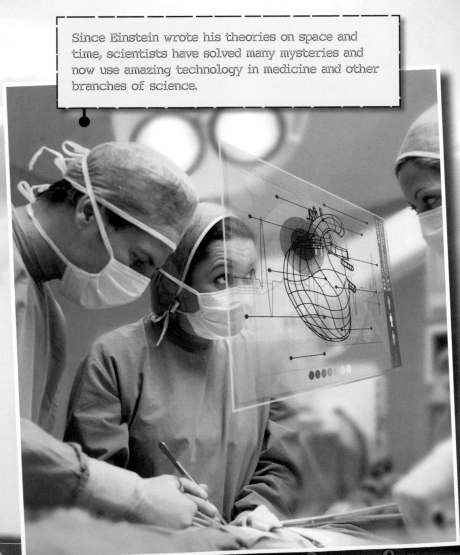

Since Einstein wrote his theories on space and time, scientists have solved many mysteries and now use amazing technology in medicine and other branches of science.

AMAZING UNIVERSE

The secrets of the Universe can be puzzling even to top scientists. New secrets like black holes and possible wormholes are being uncovered all the time.

So time travel is just one of many mysteries about the Universe that still have to be solved.

"I am enough of the artist to draw freely upon my imagination. Imagination is more important than knowledge. Knowledge is limited. Imagination encircles the world."

Albert Einstein

There is a supermassive black hole at the centre of our galaxy. It is about 4 million times the mass of the Sun. Don't worry – the black hole is no threat to Earth as it is around 26,000 light years away.

The Universe is unimaginably huge and home to at least 1,000,000,000,000,000,000,000 stars – that's a billion trillion! But the Universe is expanding all the time, with galaxies moving away from each other.

This is an image of the black hole at the centre of our Milky Way galaxy.

There is much more matter in the Universe than we can actually see. It's not that we need bigger telescopes – this matter is actually invisible and is called dark matter. Scientists are still trying to unlock the secrets of dark matter.

TIMELINE

1879
Albert Einstein is born

1905
Einstein publishes his *Special Theory of Relativity*, the theory that suggests it may be possible to move through time

1875 — 1900 — 1925 — 1950

1915
Einstein publishes the *General Theory of Relativity*, his full theory of how gravity shapes space and time

1895
H.G. Wells publishes *The Time Machine*, his story of a time traveller journeying to the future

1935
Einstein, working with Nathan Rosen, suggests the idea for what we now call wormholes

2010
Large Hadron Collider goes into full operation at CERN in Switzerland

1967
American John Wheeler becomes the first to use the phrase "black hole" to describe an area of space from which light cannot escape

1974
American Frank Tipler develops a plan for a possible time machine

1985
One of the most successful films of the year is time travel tale *Back to the Future*, featuring a time machine made from a DeLorean car

1950 **1975** **2000** **2025**

2009
Professor Stephen Hawking holds a party that only time travellers from the future would know about. Nobody comes.

1963
First broadcast of time-travelling TV series *Doctor Who*, in which the Doctor travels through time in a time machine called a TARDIS

1990
Hubble Space Telescope is placed in orbit around Earth, enabling astronomers to see distant galaxies billions of light years away. The light from these galaxies was emitted close to the birth of the Universe.

1980s
Physicist Kip Thorne, after advising Carl Sagan on a science fiction book, investigates whether it would be possible to travel through a wormhole to another area of space and time

GLOSSARY

abducted kidnapped. People who say they have been adbucted by aliens believe they have been taken on to an alien spacecraft.

accelerate increase speed or move more quickly

atom smallest particle of a chemical element that can exist from which all materials are made

axis imaginary line around which something rotates, such as a planet

bias favouring a particular point of view or opinion

black hole area of space with such a strong gravitational field that not even light can escape from it

coordinates measurements used to identify an exact position on Earth, in space and possibly in time

equator imaginary line drawn around Earth, which divides it into two equally-sized parts

event horizon boundary around a black hole, from within which no light can escape

galaxy vast collection of stars, planets, gas and other material, held together by gravity. Earth is part of the Milky Way galaxy.

gravitational field volume over which gravitational force of an object extends

gravity force that pulls objects which have mass towards each other. Big objects, such as planets, have much stronger gravity than smaller objects as the force is directly proportional to the mass of the object.

hypothesis proposed explanation for how or why something happens, which can then be tested by experiments

laboratory place where science experiments and research are carried out

mass property of matter that measures its resistance to acceleration. The mass of an object depends on the number and type of atoms in it (for example a cubic centimetre of gold will have twice the mass of a cubic centimetre of lead). The basic unit of measurement for mass is the kilogram.

matter anything that has mass and fills space, such as solids, liquids and gases

National Aeronautics and Space Administration (NASA) the part of the US Government that is responsible for exploring space

particle tiny piece of matter, such as parts that make up an atom

physicist scientist working in the subject of physics, which is the scientific study of the Universe and everything in it

science fiction writing that deals with subjects such as future worlds and alien life

speed of light speed at which light travels in a vacuum, which is always 299,792 kilometres (186,282 miles) per second

time loop scientific idea of a path through space–time in which time itself is bent into a circle, allowing a time traveller to travel through time

time zone area where clocks are set to the same time. Earth's surface is divided into 24 time zones.

vacuum space with no matter at all in it. Outer space is a vacuum.

velocity speed of movement in a particular direction

warp bend or twist

wormhole rip or hole in space which may or may not exist. Scientists believe that wormholes could make time travel possible.

FIND OUT MORE

Are you still looking for answers? You can find more about the wonders of the Universe and the possibilities of time travel in your local library, or by searching online. Here are a few ideas about where to look next.

Books

Albert Einstein and his Inflatable Universe (Horribly Famous), Dr Mike Goldsmith (Scholastic, 2010)

Really Really Big Questions about Space and Time, Mark Brake (Kingfisher, 2012)

Stephen Hawking (Inspirational Lives), Sonya Newland (Wayland, 2015)

Why Are Black Holes Black? Questions and Answers about Outer Space, Thomas Canavan (Franklin Watts, 2013)

The Time Machine, H.G. Wells (1895)

One of the most famous novels about time travel is available in many editions, including graphic novels.

Websites

Some of the ideas about time travel take a while to get your head around. These websites offer some detailed explanations.

www.bbc.co.uk/programmes/p01tlhsc

In this video clip, Professor Brian Cox explains how black holes alter space and time.

www.cernland.net

Discover more about the Large Hadron Collider on CERN's website for young people.

www.easyscienceforkids.com/all-about-black-holes/

This website gives simple, understandable information about black holes, including an animated video and fun facts.

www.sciencekids.co.nz/videos/physics/timetravel.html
This cool website has a video in which famous physicist Michio Kaku
explains some of the exciting time travel possibilities that appear in the film
Back to the Future, and why going forwards in time would be much easier
than going back.

spaceplace.nasa.gov/review/dr-marc-space/time-travel.html
This blog post from NASA explores whether time travel is possible.

Exploring further
You'll be able to find lots of wild ideas online about the possibilities of time
travel. Some of these ideas are put forward or supported by the world's
leading scientists and are based on the work of Einstein and others. Other
ideas may not be quite so reliable, such as the scientists who believed that
the Large Hadron Collider could create a large black hole and cause the end
of the world.

Sources of information you can trust include NASA or leading universities,
as well as journals and news sources such as the BBC or National
Geographic.

Science fiction and films
Time travel is the basis for many different science fiction stories and films.
Some of the most famous are the *Back to the Future* films. These can be
great fun, but if you've learned anything from your search for clues, don't
make the mistake of thinking they are telling the truth about time travel.

INDEX